AMERICAN BULLFROGS

by Katie Marsico

Children's Press®

An Imprint of Scholastic Inc.
New York Toronto London Auckland Sydney
Mexico City New Delhi Hong Kong
Danbury, Connecticut

Content Consultant
Dr. Stephen S. Ditchkoff
Professor of Wildlife Sciences
Auburn University
Auburn, Alabama

Photographs © 2013: age fotostock: 39 (B Trapp/Blickwinkel), 8
(Bruce Corbett/All Canada Photos), 20 (FLPA/Treat Davidson); Andy
Fyon/www.ontariowildflower.com: 27; Bob Italiano: 44 foreground,
45 foreground; Dreamstime: 2 background, 3 background, 44
background, 45 background (Benjshepherd), cover (Mirceax);
iStockphoto: 7 (Chris Hill), 24 (Robin Arnold); Media Bakery: 15
(Gary Neil Corbett), 11 (Jeremy Woodhouse); Photo Researchers: 23
(Dante Fenolio), 19 (Ken Thomas), 4, 5 background, 35, 40 (Kenneth
H. Thomas), 5 top, 32 (Paul Whitten), 31 (Volker Steger); Shutterstock,
Inc.: 12 (Anna Hoychuk), 1, 2 foreground, 3 foreground, 46 (Gerald
A. DeBoer); Superstock, Inc.: 5 bottom, 28, 36 (Animals Animals), 16
(imagebroker.net).

Library of Congress Cataloging-in-Publication Data
Marsico, Katie, 1980–
    American Bullfrogs/by Katie Marsico.
        p. cm.—(Nature's children)
    Includes bibliographical references and index.
    ISBN-13: 978-0-531-26832-2 (lib. bdg.)
    ISBN-13: 978-0-531-25477-6 (pbk.)
1. Bullfrog—Juvenile literature. I. Title.
    QL668.E27M34 2013
    597.8'92—dc23
    2012000645

All rights reserved. Published in 2013 by Children's Press, an imprint
of Scholastic Inc.
Printed in China 62
SCHOLASTIC, CHILDREN'S PRESS, and associated logos are
trademarks and/or registered trademarks of Scholastic Inc.

1 2 3 4 5 6 7 8 9 10 R 22 21 20 19 18 17 16 15 14 13

American Bullfrogs

Class	Amphibia
Order	Anura
Families	Ranidae
Genus	*Rana*
Species	*Rana catesbeiana*
World distribution	Wetlands throughout North America, South America, southern Europe, and Asia
Habitats	Warm, shallow waters in streams, rivers, ponds, lakes, marshes, and bogs
Distinctive physical characteristics	Adults have moist skin that is brown, gray, or green; large, bulging eyes; no outer ears; powerful, long hind legs; webbed hind toes; wide mouth that features a strong tongue and an upper row of teeth; tadpoles have gills that are used for breathing, no legs, and a long tail
Habits	Breathes using both lungs and skin; communicates vocally; hunts ferociously and feeds on almost anything it can fit inside its mouth; is mainly solitary; mates about once a year; spends most of its time in the water
Diet	Carnivorous; feeds on insects, fish, the eggs of other aquatic animals, small snakes, turtles, mice, birds, baby alligators, and even other frogs; tadpoles mainly eat aquatic plants

AMERICAN BULLFROGS

Contents

CHAPTER 1

A Bellow Across the Bog

As evening arrives, silence seems to set in over the waters of a bog. Then suddenly the quiet is shattered by a rumbling noise that sounds like a cow bellowing. That's no farm animal echoing across the wetland. It is a male American bullfrog calling into the night air.

American bullfrogs are the largest frogs in North America. These sizable amphibians also exist across several other parts of the globe. They all live in freshwater environments.

Bullfrogs are carnivores. This means they only eat meat. They are highly skilled hunters. These large frogs know how to remain still as they patiently wait for prey to move in their direction. Once a bullfrog spies an insect or small bird—or sometimes even an unsuspecting snake or baby alligator—it lunges forward and gobbles the animal down.

Bullfrogs are powerful jumpers. They can spring forward 3 to 6 feet (0.9 to 1.8 meters) in a single leap! This makes them impressive to many people.

The bullfrog's size and loud bellow set it apart from other frogs.

A Single Species

The word *bullfrog* is often used to describe several types of larger frogs all over the world. The giant bullfrog in Australia and the crowned bullfrog in Africa are two examples of this. So are the Indus Valley bullfrog and the banded bullfrog of Asia. However, most scientists believe that there is only one true species of bullfrog—the American bullfrog.

American bullfrogs are also often confused with green frogs. Both types of frogs look similar, but American bullfrogs are bigger and make longer, deeper calls. Green frogs also have a ridge that wraps around each of their eardrums and runs down their backs. In American bullfrogs, this ridge does not stretch past the eardrums. Finally, most people do not think green frogs pose the same threat to the natural environment as their larger relatives do.

FUN FACT! Bullfrogs got their name because their calls sound so much like those of bull cattle.

Green frogs look a lot like smaller bullfrogs.

CHAPTER 2

Survival in the Swamp

One of an American bullfrog's most noticeable physical features is its size. These huge frogs sometimes weigh up to 1.5 pounds (0.7 kilograms) and have been known to measure 8 inches (20 centimeters) from nose to **rump**. On average, however, most weigh roughly 1.1 pounds (0.5 kg) and stretch 3.5 to 6 inches (9 to 15 cm) long. These measurements do not include the length of a bullfrog's hind legs.

Their size gives them an advantage over smaller amphibians that sometimes have a harder time defending themselves against **predators**. If a bullfrog senses danger or is afraid, it often sucks in air. This causes its body to swell so that it appears even larger.

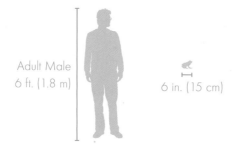

Adult Male
6 ft. (1.8 m)

6 in. (15 cm)

Bullfrogs can make themselves look much bigger than they actually are.

Skin That Serves Many Purposes

A bullfrog's skin is another important feature that helps it survive in the wild. It helps the frog blend in with its environment. A bullfrog's skin is usually colored in various shades of green, gray, and brown. This natural camouflage makes the frogs less visible when they are surrounded by water, rocks, mud, and aquatic plants.

Bullfrogs rely on their skin to do far more than just blend into the wetlands around them. Like all amphibians, they also use it to breathe. Bullfrogs take in some air with their lungs, but they also soak up oxygen through their skin. They absorb water this way, too, since they do not use their mouths to drink water like people do. The bullfrog's skin is most absorbent when it is wet. That is why these frogs spend almost all of their time in the water.

Bullfrogs usually keep their eyes and nostrils above the water so they can see and breathe.

Poisonous and Replaceable

The bullfrog's skin also contains special **glands** that are filled with toxins, or poisons. The frogs can release the toxins when they are in danger. This comes in handy when they realize enemies are close by and want to keep them at a distance!

Because a bullfrog's skin serves so many purposes, it is important that it remains healthy. Shedding old skin about once a week helps accomplish this goal. Like many other frogs, a bullfrog sheds by opening its mouth as wide as it can while stretching out the rest of its body. This loosens any dead skin on the frog's body.

The bullfrog pulls at the loosened skin with its legs. It then shoves the skin into its mouth and eats it! Meanwhile, the bullfrog uncovers a layer of fresh, new skin that helps it breathe, absorb water, and fend off predators.

A bullfrog's skin is one of its most important features.

Exceptional Senses

Bullfrogs also depend a great deal on their large, bulging eyes. They have a remarkable sense of vision and are able to detect different colors. Bullfrogs can see in several directions at once and have excellent **depth perception.**

A bullfrog's eyes and nose are both positioned along the top of its head. Bullfrogs can breathe and watch what is going on around them without having to move completely out of the water. This allows them to stay hidden as they quietly wait for prey to pass by.

Bullfrogs have a keen sense of hearing, too. Unlike humans and many other animals, they do not have outer ears. Instead, they have large circles located just behind their eyes. These are eardrums that prevent water and dirt from seeping into their inner ears.

A bullfrog's bulging eyes allow it to see above water while remaining hidden from prey.

A Hunter's Mighty Mouth

Besides being skilled survivors, bullfrogs are ferocious hunters. They devour almost any animal they can fit inside their mouths. Bullfrogs have a powerful, muscular tongue that they use to snap up prey. In some cases, they also use their front legs, or forepaws, to force larger animals into their jaws.

Tiny, sharp teeth line the roofs of their mouths but are rarely needed to tear apart food. Bullfrogs usually swallow their meals whole. They often use their teeth to clamp down on struggling prey. These huge frogs frequently kill other animals by suffocating them, or cutting off their air supply.

Sometimes bullfrogs **submerge** and pull their captured prey underwater. Land animals that need oxygen to survive put up less of a fight once they are dragged underwater. Unlike many other frogs, bullfrogs are also capable of catching and killing many types of aquatic prey such as fish.

A bullfrog can use its tongue to flip prey into its open mouth.

Jumpers and Swimmers

A bullfrog's powerful hind legs can add an extra 7 to 10 inches (18 to 25 cm) to its total length. These long, strong legs allow the frogs to jump incredible distances to escape predators and capture prey. Bullfrogs have been known to leap up to nine times their body length. That would be like an adult man jumping more than 50 feet (15 m)!

Bullfrogs also use their hind legs to swim through the water. They use their forepaws to steer and change direction. Like other aquatic frogs, bullfrogs have webbed feet. A thin layer of skin connects the toes on each hind foot. This allows bullfrogs to move their feet like paddles and increase their swimming speed.

FUN FACT! Bullfrog legs are a popular food in some parts of the world, including China, France, and the southern United States.

Bullfrogs are excellent swimmers.

CHAPTER 3

Life in the Water

American bullfrogs are found in many different freshwater environments all over North America. These large amphibians live as far north as Canada and as far south as Mexico. They have **adapted** to life across most parts of the United States as well. Over time, humans have brought them to Europe, South America, and Asia.

Bullfrogs live in streams, rivers, ponds, lakes, marshes, and bogs. They usually seek out areas that have warm, shallow water. Frogs are cold-blooded. This means that the outside environment affects their body temperature.

Bullfrogs **hibernate** when the weather grows colder. Their body systems slow down, and they become less active. Because their bodies use less energy, they do not need as much food. During winter, many bullfrogs build small underwater caves out of mud, and they hibernate in them until it is warmer. They continue to get oxygen from the water around them as it passes over their skin.

When hibernating, bullfrogs often stay hidden in the mud until spring.

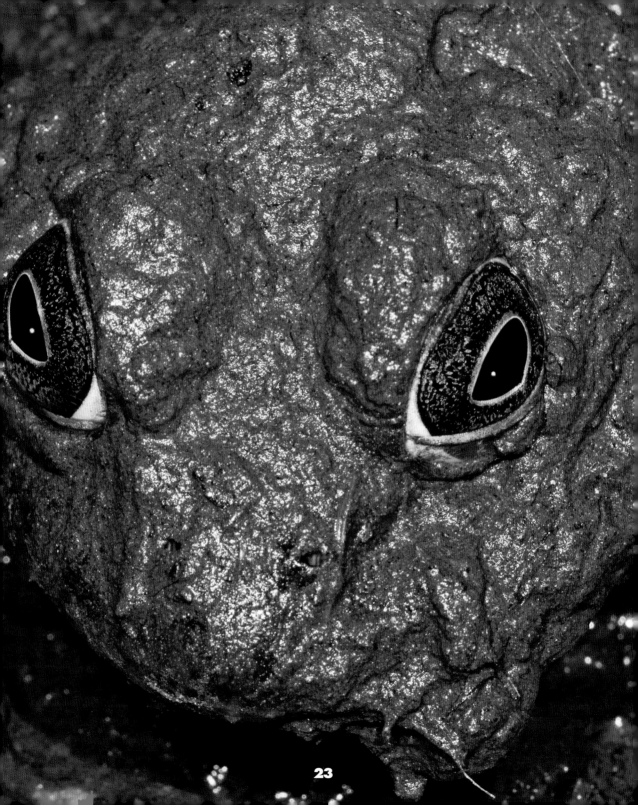

Both Predators and Prey

Bullfrogs eat a wide variety of foods. Insects, fish, and the eggs of other aquatic animals are just a few of the foods that make up their diet. They also have been known to feed on small snakes, turtles, mice, birds, and even baby alligators. They often eat other frogs. Usually, the frogs are of different species, but sometimes bullfrogs even eat each other!

Bullfrogs search for their next meal throughout all hours of the day and night, but scientists suspect that they are most active in the evening. Since they are cold-blooded, warmer weather tends to increase their appetites.

Bullfrogs are not only predators—they are also prey. Birds such as herons, egrets, and kingfishers hunt them. So do raccoons, turtles, and snakes. These creatures tend to go after younger, smaller bullfrogs because they are easier to catch and kill.

Bullfrogs make tasty meals for birds such as great blue herons.

Bullfrog Behavior

Bullfrogs are usually solitary animals. They prefer to live alone and are very territorial. These amphibians use chirps, squeaks, grunts, and bellows to communicate with one another about possible danger or to attract a mate. They make similar noises to protect their territory. Bullfrogs quickly become aggressive if they sense that another bullfrog is trying to invade their space.

One exception to this rule occurs when the frogs come together to mate and produce young. Bullfrogs are typically ready to mate when they are between three and five years old. Females sometimes lay up to 20,000 eggs after mating!

At first, this large group of eggs floats in a jellylike sheet near the surface of the water. Eventually it sinks, until it rests on nearby aquatic plants. The eggs hatch about three to five days later. By then, the mother is long gone. The newborn frogs are left to survive on their own.

Bullfrogs lay their tiny eggs in huge groups.

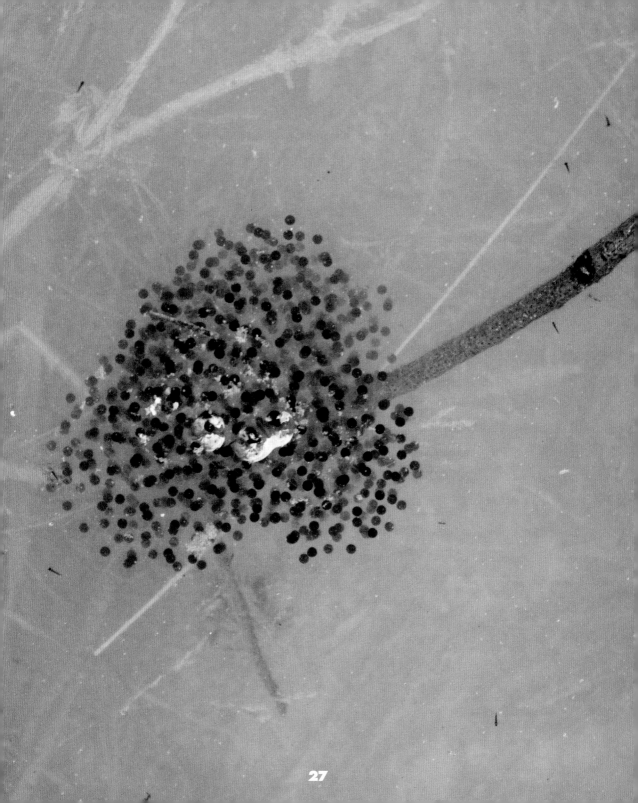

From Tadpole to Adult

Baby bullfrogs look quite different than they do as adults. Like other amphibians, bullfrogs go through a **larval** stage. During this time, they are known as tadpoles. These young bullfrogs have a tail but no legs. They rely on **gills** to breathe instead of lungs.

Bullfrog tadpoles measure less than 0.2 inches (0.5 cm) long when they first hatch. They are not the aggressive hunters they will become later in life. Most bullfrog tadpoles start off eating aquatic plants. They can swim but are not incredibly active. This helps them avoid attracting the attention of predators such as birds, fish, snakes, and turtles.

Over time, bullfrog tadpoles lose their tails and grow legs. They also learn to breathe using lungs instead of gills. It can take up to three years for a tadpole to develop into an adult bullfrog. In the wild, these frogs usually live for about seven to nine years.

In some ways, young tadpoles look more like fish than frogs.

CHAPTER 4

Bullfrogs Throughout History

Amphibians have lived on Earth for more than 350 million years. This means they existed roughly 100 million years before dinosaurs roamed the planet. Their earliest ancestors were probably fish. Fossils reveal that early amphibians that look most similar to modern frogs date back approximately 180 million years.

Over time, these early frogs continued to grow and change. The family of frogs to which bullfrogs belong appeared between 56 million and 34 million years ago. Experts are less clear about when modern bullfrogs first appeared.

Scientists started formally describing American bullfrogs by name in 1802. They know that bullfrogs were at first only native to the central and eastern wetlands of North America. Humans eventually introduced them to other parts of the world.

Fossils have helped scientists learn about bullfrogs and their ancestors.

Frog Invaders

During the 1920s and 1930s, settlers in the American West relied on frogs for food. Eventually, people in the eastern United States started shipping bullfrogs to western areas to feed the growing demand for frog meat. Some even opened bullfrog farms. It was not uncommon for these frogs to escape and adapt to life in the wild.

In many cases, these bullfrogs invaded fish **hatcheries**. Government officials trying to reintroduce certain fish, such as trout, to rivers and lakes were not always aware of this fact. They unintentionally dumped bullfrog tadpoles into nonnative wetlands when they brought in fish from the hatcheries.

Bullfrogs also spread across North America, southern Europe, South America, and Asia for other reasons. Some were **imported** to be sold in pet stores. Others were moved to nonnative areas where people hunted them for sport or used them to control insect populations.

American bullfrogs can now be found in many areas where they do not belong.

Thriving in New Environments

Thanks to their incredible survival skills, American bullfrogs had no trouble adapting to their new homes in nonnative areas. Unlike other frog species, bullfrogs have no trouble living in waters warmer than those found in their native habitats. It is also easy for them to survive because these new environments lack many of the predators that control bullfrog populations in their natural homes.

Without any real threats to survival, nonnative bullfrogs can multiply much more quickly than they can in native habitats. Once they mate, even just a few frogs can rapidly produce tens of thousands of eggs. More tadpoles are able to survive to adulthood because there are fewer predators to lower their numbers.

FUN FACT! In some nonnative areas, bullfrogs thrive because the native fish do not like the taste of bullfrog tadpoles.

American bullfrogs can thrive and grow in many different environments.

CHAPTER 5

Preventing Future Dangers

Scientists are busily working with government leaders and the public to protect countless plant and animal species that are in danger of dying out. They tend to have a slightly different goal when it comes to bullfrogs. They are struggling to prevent these amphibians from invading nonnative wetlands all over the world.

American bullfrogs often cause major problems for other wildlife when they enter new areas. Their huge appetites are a big part of the issue. Bullfrogs begin competing with native species for food. They also spread diseases. This eventually hurts other animal populations. The bullfrog's growing presence may be enough to wipe out species that are already endangered.

Leopard frogs are among the many frog species affected by invasive American bullfrogs.

The Benefits of Bullfrogs

Invasive bullfrogs frequently have a negative effect on wetland environments. On the other hand, they can sometimes have a positive impact on the world around them. For example, bullfrogs help control insect pests such as mosquitoes.

Mosquitoes tend to reproduce near water, where frogs spend most of their time. These insects spread diseases to both people and animals. Bullfrogs feed on mosquitoes, helping to limit their numbers.

Human beings depend on bullfrogs for more than just insect control. Scientists often study these frogs when they carry out research. The bullfrog's body systems work a lot like those of more complex animals. Many researchers view these frogs' bodies as simpler versions of larger species—including human beings! Another reason scientists like to use bullfrogs in scientific research is that they are smaller and easier to care for than bigger animals such as monkeys.

People need to do more to prevent bullfrogs from spreading to nonnative areas.

The Part People Can Play

The benefits of bullfrogs have encouraged human beings to search for solutions to the problems that these amphibians sometimes pose to the environment. One of the best ways to stop the spread of any invasive species is to educate the public. Many people are unaware of the effects that nonnative bullfrogs have on other animals. Fortunately, people are learning to be more aware of these frogs and are working harder to keep them away from areas where they do not belong.

People are also making more of an effort to avoid polluting waterways. Pollution tends to raise water temperatures and boosts the growth of certain aquatic plants. This creates the type of living space that bullfrogs prefer. Scientists do not want these interesting amphibians to completely take over every wetland environment. However, they are eager to find new ways to create the perfect balance between American bullfrogs and the natural world around them.

Without our help, nonnative bullfrogs could cause major problems in environments throughout North America.

Words to Know

adapted (uh-DAPT-id) — changed in order to fit a new setting or set of circumstances

aggressive (uh-GRESS-iv) — ready to fight or attack

amphibians (am-FIB-ee-uhnz) — animals that have backbones and live in water and breathe with gills when young; as adults, they develop lungs and live on land

aquatic (uh-KWAH-tik) — living or growing in water

bellowing (BEH-low-ing) — making a loud, deep noise similar to the sounds a cow often produces

bog (BAWG) — a marshy, moss-filled wetland

camouflage (KAM-o-flaj) — coloring or body shape that allows an animal to blend in with its surroundings

depth perception (DEPTH pur-SEP-shuhn) — the ability to detect how near or far various objects are

eardrums (EER-druhmz) — thin sheets of skin that make up part of the ear and vibrate in response to sound signals

endangered (en-DAYN-jurd) — at risk of becoming extinct, usually because of human activity

environments (en-VYE-ruhn-mints) — surroundings in which an animal lives or spends time

family (FAM-uh-lee) — a group of living things that are related to each other

fossils (FOSS-uhlz) — the hardened remains of prehistoric plants and animals

gills (GILZ) — organs that remove oxygen from water to help fish and other underwater animals breathe

glands (GLANDZ) — organs in the body that produce natural chemicals

hatcheries (HA-chuh-reez) — places where fish eggs are hatched outside of their natural environment

hibernate (HYE-bur-nate) — to sleep through the winter in order to survive when temperatures are cold and food is hard to find

imported (im-PORT-id) — brought into a place or country from somewhere else

invasive (in-VAY-siv) — describing a plant or animal that is introduced to a new habitat and may cause that habitat harm

larval (LAHR-vuhl) — describing an early life stage that occurs between the time amphibians hatch and when they transform into adults

mate (MAYT) — an animal that joins with another animal to reproduce

native (NAY-tiv) — naturally belonging to a certain place

polluting (puh-LOO-ting) — damaging or contaminating the air, water, and soil

predators (PREH-duh-turz) — animals that live by hunting other animals for food

prey (PRAY) — an animal that's hunted by another animal for food

rump (RUHMP) — the hind part of an animal's body

species (SPEE-sheez) — one of the groups into which animals and plants of the same genus are divided

submerge (suhb-MURJ) — to sink below the surface of the water

territorial (terr-uh-TOR-ee-uhl) — defensive of a certain area

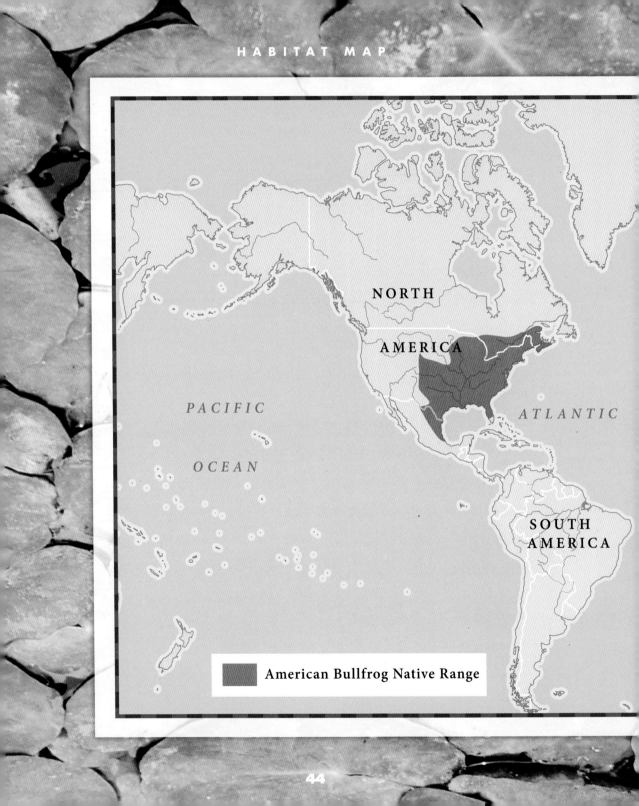

NORTH

AMERICA

PACIFIC

OCEAN

ATLANTIC

SOUTH
AMERICA

American Bullfrog Native Range

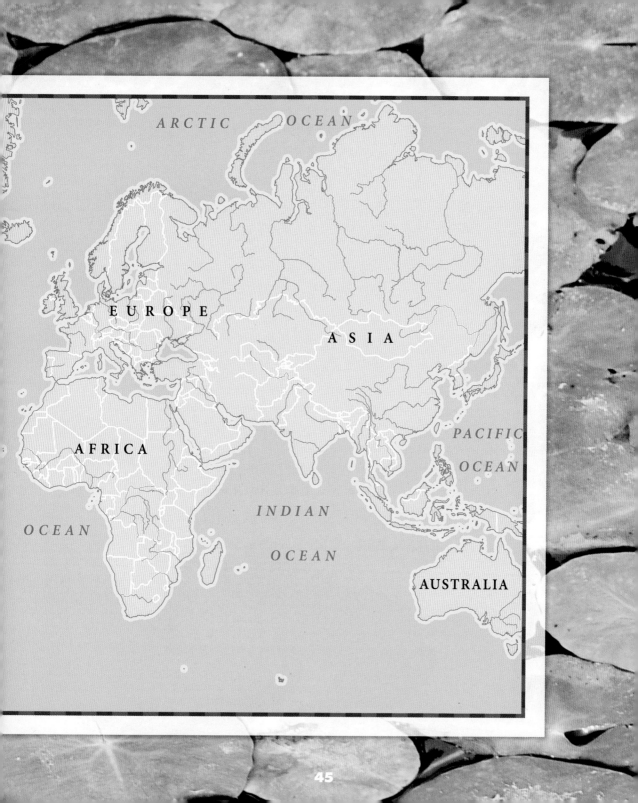

Find Out More

Books
Bishop, Nic. *Frogs*. New York: Scholastic, 2008.

Gray, Susan H. *Bullfrog*. Ann Arbor, MI: Cherry Lake Publishing, 2009.

Perkins, Wendy. *Frog*. Mankato, MN: Amicus, 2012.

Turner, Pamela S. *The Frog Scientist*. Boston: Houghton Mifflin, 2009.

Zemlicka, Shannon. *From Tadpole to Frog*. Minneapolis: Lerner Publications Company, 2012.

Visit this Scholastic Web site for more information on American bullfrogs:
www.factsfornow.scholastic.com
Enter the keyword **Bullfrogs**

Index

About the Author

Katie Marsico is the author of more than 100 children's books. Once the weather warms up, she intends to see if she and her kids can spot any bullfrogs in the creek near their house outside of Chicago, Illinois.

DATE DUE

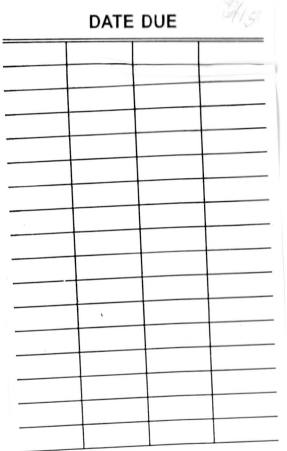

Demco, Inc. 38-293